How Does Your Garden Grow?

Be Your Own Plant Expert

Dominique and Philippe Joly
Nathalie Locoste, Jean-Claude Senée

Sterling Publishing Co., Inc.   New York

Text by Dominique and Philippe Joly
Illustrated by Nathalie Locoste and Jean-Claude Senée
Translated by Fay Greenbaum; English edition edited by Isabel Stein

Library of Congress Cataloging-in-Publication Data

Joly, Dominique.
    [Découvre les plantes et crée ton jardin. English]
    How does your garden grow?: be your own plant expert / Dominique & Philippe Joly;
[illustrations by] Nathalie Locoste & Jean-Claude Senée; [translated by Fay Greenbaum].
        p.   cm.
    Includes index.
    Summary: Follows the process of gardening from the definition and description of a plant,
botanical experiments, types of gardens, to preparation and maintenance.
    ISBN 0-8069-6133-3
    1. Gardening—Juvenile literature.   2. Botany—Experiments—Juvenile literature.
[1. Gardening. 2. Plants—Experiments. 3. Botany—Experiments. 4. Experiments.] I. Joly,
Philippe.   II. Locoste, Nathalie, ill.   III. Jean-Claude Senée, ill.   IV. Title.
SB457.J6413   1996
581—dc20   96-26122
                                                                                      CIP
                                                                                       AC

10 9 8 7 6 5 4 3 2 1

Published 1996 by Sterling Publishing Company, Inc.
387 Park Avenue South, New York, N.Y. 10016
First published in France by Éditions Mango
under the title *Découvre les Plantes et Crée Ton Jardin*
by Dominique and Philippe Joly, Nathalie Locoste, and Jean-Claude Senée
© 1994 by Éditions Mango
English translation © 1996 by Sterling Publishing Company
Distributed in Canada by Sterling Publishing
⁒ Canadian Manda Group, One Atlantic Avenue, Suite 105
Toronto, Ontario, Canada M6K 3E7
Printed in Hong Kong
All rights reserved

Sterling ISBN 0-8069-6133-3

CONTENTS

CREATE YOUR OWN GARDEN

In the wild or in a garden, reaching up toward the sky or spread out along the ground, edible or poisonous, plants come in a great variety of shapes and colors. Given a little moisture, warmth, and light, they manage to grow. Discover their changing smell, touch their leaves, listen to their noises, and taste their fruit. You will want to grow them in order to see their life cycle as the days go by.

FROM NOMADIC HUNTER TO FARMER

The first people wandered in search of food; they lived by hunting, fishing and gathering. Little by little, over about 10 000 years, they changed their way of life. From nomadic hunters, people became farmers and breeders of livestock, raising wild grains (wheat, barley, rice, or corn) and harvesting them from year to year.

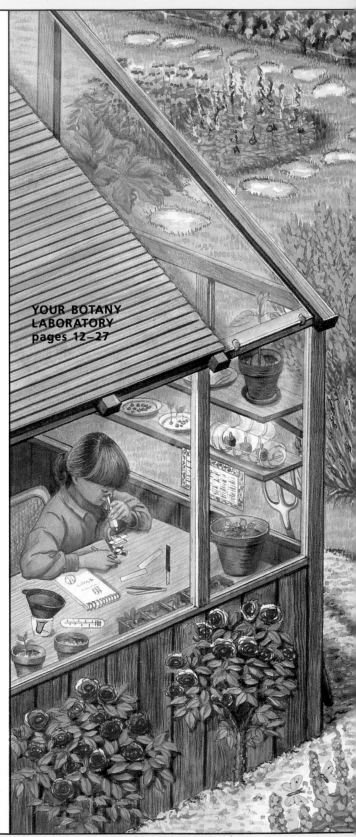

YOUR BOTANY LABORATORY pages 12–27

WHAT IS A PLANT?
pages 8–11

PREPARING YOUR GARDEN
pages 28–41

WHAT IS A PLANT?

There are more than 300 000 species of plants. Trees, mosses, ferns, and flowering plants all belong to the immense plant kingdom. Whether gripping the slopes of snowy mountains or buried in desert sands, plants have some things in common: for the most part, they are green, attached to the ground, and manufacture their own food, using sunlight. Most living things depend on them to survive; plants are the guardians of life on Earth.

THE STEM

The stem holds the buds, branches, leaves, flowers, and fruit. It contains vascular tissues that ensure the circulation of the sap.

ABOVE GROUND

twining stem of the convolvulus

stolons of the strawberry

tree trunk

UNDERGROUND STEMS

tubers (potatoes)

rhizome of lily of the valley

hyacinth bulb

A flower grows from a bud on a stem. The flower is the plant's reproductive organ (see pp. 22–23). After it is fertilized, the flower develops into a fruit, which contains seeds.

The leaves manufacture substances that nourish the plant and make it grow (see p. 20).

The roots, generally underground, are the parts that anchor the plant to the ground. They draw up water and nutrients the plant needs through the root hairs.

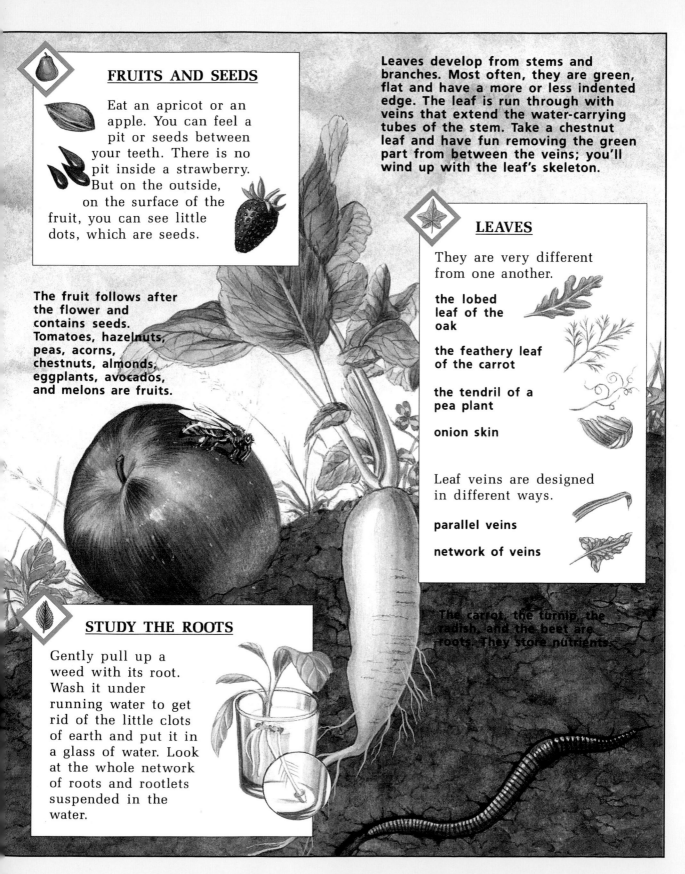

FRUITS AND SEEDS

Eat an apricot or an apple. You can feel a pit or seeds between your teeth. There is no pit inside a strawberry. But on the outside, on the surface of the fruit, you can see little dots, which are seeds.

The fruit follows after the flower and contains seeds. Tomatoes, hazelnuts, peas, acorns, chestnuts, almonds, eggplants, avocados, and melons are fruits.

Leaves develop from stems and branches. Most often, they are green, flat and have a more or less indented edge. The leaf is run through with veins that extend the water-carrying tubes of the stem. Take a chestnut leaf and have fun removing the green part from between the veins; you'll wind up with the leaf's skeleton.

LEAVES

They are very different from one another.

the lobed leaf of the oak

the feathery leaf of the carrot

the tendril of a pea plant

onion skin

Leaf veins are designed in different ways.

parallel veins

network of veins

The carrot, the turnip, the radish, and the beet are roots. They store nutrients.

STUDY THE ROOTS

Gently pull up a weed with its root. Wash it under running water to get rid of the little clots of earth and put it in a glass of water. Look at the whole network of roots and rootlets suspended in the water.

THE DIVERSITY OF LIFE

You will find many different kinds of living things in the garden. You may find some that are like the ones on this page. Scientists study and classify living things into categories. From largest to smallest categories: kingdom, phylum, class, order, family, genus, and species.

1. Mushrooms are fungi; they do not have chlorophyll or make their own food, so they are not true plants.

2. Algae are one-celled or many-celled, plantlike, and almost all live in water.

3. A lichen is a combination of a fungus and an alga, growing together.

4. Bryophytes (liverworts and mosses) are small green plants without true leaves and conducting tissues.

5. Ferns have conducting tissues (they are tracheophytes), but need water for fertilization.

6. Angiosperms, the flowering plants, carry seeds enclosed in an ovary.

7. Gymnosperms carry their seeds on the scales of cones.

EXTRACTING CHLOROPHYLL

Plants owe their green color to a pigment, chlorophyll. Xanthophyll and carotene are other pigments found in plants, which give them colors ranging from yellow to red. These two pigments are most frequently hidden by the green color of chlorophyll. In autumn, the chlorophyll disappears from the leaves and it no longer hides the other colors.

Separate the chlorophyll from the other pigments

Take a few fresh spinach leaves; chop them up in a blender or food mill.

Pour a little rubbing alcohol on the chopped leaves and mix. Pour your preparation through a coffee filter and collect the green liquid.

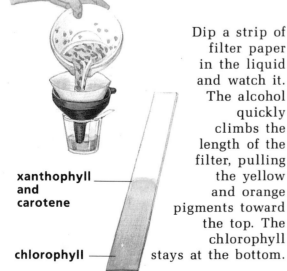

Dip a strip of filter paper in the liquid and watch it. The alcohol quickly climbs the length of the filter, pulling the yellow and orange pigments toward the top. The chlorophyll stays at the bottom.

xanthophyll and carotene

chlorophyll

THE COMPOSITION OF PLANTS

Plant matter is made of cells, which contain a great deal of water.

Leeks, mushrooms, and lettuce are 85% to 95% water.

Weigh out 2 oz. or 50 g of lettuce leaves. Cut them in pieces and put them in a saucepan and heat them; watch the steam that is released. Weigh what is left and calculate how much weight has been lost.

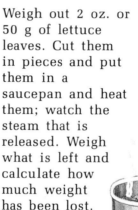

DID YOU KNOW?

Chlorophyll has the power to absorb bad odors. This is why it is included in some toothpastes and chewing gums.

YOUR BOTANY LABORATORY

In order to become more familiar with the plant world, make a botany laboratory in a sheltered spot. By doing experiments and culturing things, you will better understand the work of the roots, leaves, stem and flowers, each of which helps in its own way in plant growth or reproduction.

LEARNING TO USE A MICROSCOPE

Start by adjusting the mirror or light so that your object is well lit. Looking at the microscope from the side, lower the lens as close as possible to the glass slide, but watch carefully to avoid hitting the slide. Put your eye to the eyepiece and gradually raise the tube back up until the image is completely in focus. Adjust the mirror or light again to get the best possible light.

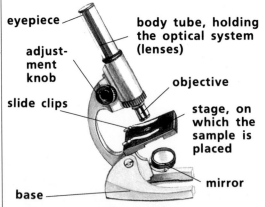

eyepiece

body tube, holding the optical system (lenses)

adjustment knob

objective

slide clips

stage, on which the sample is placed

mirror

base

Place your mounted slides and your test cultures on shelves in the light.

Take a spider plant cutting (see p. 26)

Watch water circulate through a plant (see p. 16)

Discover the basic needs of a plant (see p.14—15)

Observe how the roots grow downwards (see p. 19)

Make an avocado pit grow (see p. 24)

Look at the stomates of a leek (see p. 19)

Put in a large, solid table on which you can put your microscope, do experiments, and take notes in your laboratory. Cover it with a dark, waterproof tablecloth. Sit in a comfortable chair to make your observations and wear a cotton shirt or apron.

Put the materials you will use often at arm's reach: a roll of paper towels, tweezers, an eyedropper, a notebook and pen.

SOME THINGS TO LOOK AT

All your specimens for slides should be very thin, almost transparent. An enlargement of 200 times (200×) should be enough to study them.

fine cactus spines

stinging hairs of the nettle

feathery seeds of the dandelion

anthers of a flower

pollen grains

mushroom spores

Wipe the lenses of your microscope with a clean handkerchief before and after use. Clean and put away the slides and slide covers after use. You can examine other objects by slicing them very thin, which is a bit difficult, as it requires sharp instruments (razor blades, craft knife).

PRECAUTIONS

Ask an adult to help you use cutting tools such as a craft knife. Close all bottles of chemicals tightly after each use.

PLANTS NEED LIGHT

Force a runner bean sprout to find its path to the light by placing obstacles before it. It will always manage to get past them!

Place a shoe box on its side so that its cover is vertical. Cut an opening in what is now the top side (see figure).

Prepare two pieces of cardboard by cutting a hole in a different place on each. Attach the first piece of cardboard part of the way up the box, inside, as shown.

Place a pot of earth enclosing a runner bean in the bottom of the box, to the left.

Put the cover back on the box and place it in a warm, sunny spot. Water the pot regularly.

When the shoot passes through the hole, put the second piece of cardboard in place. Place the hole on the opposite side from the first one.

The shoot will change direction in order to pass through the second round hole. It will end up by growing out of the opening at the top of the box.

PLANTS NEED WATER

Soak three handfuls of lentils overnight in a salad bowl full of water. Then strain them and rinse them. Place a paper napkin folded in four in each of three saucers and put a handful of lentils on each.

AFTER SEVERAL DAYS

Saucer 1	Saucer 2	Saucer 3	Saucer 1	Saucer 2	Saucer 3

Pour in a little water every day.	**Cover the lentils completely with water.**	**Don't put in any water.**	The regularly watered lentils have sprouted.	The lentils immersed in water suffocate from lack of oxygen and rot.	There is no change in the lentils without water.

AT THE START OF THE EXPERIMENT

14

DID YOU KNOW?

Indoors, green plants always turn their leaves toward the light. In the forest, trees grow very tall to go toward the light. When a small tree finds itself next to a large one, it tries to move away.

DID YOU KNOW?

Flowers of the sunflower plant try to get maximum sunlight. Following the Sun, they change position and pull their stems along. In the evening, the stem is twisted around itself in a spiral. In the morning, it is untwisted, ready to follow the Sun again.

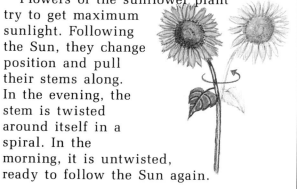

DORMANCY

Like hibernating animals, certain plants lead a slower life in winter. This is their period of dormancy, which generally starts when the days get shorter in autumn. The sap is held in reserve and causes the buds to come out in the spring.

PLANTS NEED WARMTH

Pick a few forsythia branches on which the flowers are still in bud, and put them in a vase in the house.

A forsythia branch on the bush, in the cold, does not yet have flowers.

The same branch, picked and placed in a vase in the house, develops flowers in a few days.

IN CONCLUSION

Through all of these experiments, you have seen evidence of the basic conditions needed for plant life. They need light (they die in darkness); water (they must be watered when there is not enough rain, otherwise they will dry out); and a small amount of warmth. Despite this, certain plants are amazingly adaptable; some survive deep in the desert, without water; others have to keep themselves alive under conditions of high altitude or extreme cold (see p. 17).

WHAT IS OSMOSIS?

Plants take in the nutrients they need from the soil through their roots. The passage of these nutrients from the soil in the roots occurs because of osmosis.

Because of the difference in the concentration of water molecules in the soil and in the roots, the root cells attract the water and mineral salts contained in the soil and allow them to pass into the roots.

An experiment with a carrot, powdered sugar, and a glass of water.

Hollow out a little of the inside of a carrot (see picture). Fill the hollow with powdered sugar. Put the carrot partway into a glass of water; hold it in place with wooden matches or toothpicks.

Only half the carrot should be in the water. Several hours later, the hollow will be full of water. The water moved inside the carrot to dilute the sugar.

A hollowed-out carrot, under the same conditions but without sugar, does not draw the water into the hollow.

TRANSPORT IN PLANTS

The water and mineral salts absorbed by the roots move towards the leaves.

Put a white flower (such as a lily, arum lily, or carnation) in a glass; pour in some water tinted with blue dye (methylene blue or blue ink). After a few hours, look at the petals; they will be colored blue.

Place an *Impatiens* stem in a glass of water colored red with eosin or red ink. After a few hours, you will see the red liquid showing through the stem. The water and the dye absorbed by the plant travel up into the leaves.

The water rises and is transported through the stem. The stem conducts the water to the petals.

PLANTS IN EXTREME ENVIRONMENTS

Some environments are very hostile to plants: high altitudes; cold, windy places; very dry places; and ones with high concentrations of salt in the soil, such as sea shores. Plants have made many adaptations to survive despite everything; they grow very long roots, reduce their size, form cushions, protect themselves with thorns, and coat themselves with waterproof coverings in order to hold on to their water or filter out the sun's rays.

COLD ENVIRONMENTS AT HIGH ALTITUDES

Edelweiss

Compact and small, it has a feltlike coating on its leaves, stem and flowers that protects it from the cold and reduces evaporation. The flowers, small and pressed against one another, form a capitulum (rounded head).

Edelweiss

Xanthoria

It grows on bare rocks at an altitude of up to 26 000 ft. (8 000 m). It is a lichen (see p. 10). It is capable of surviving drought and great cold.

Xanthoria

DRY ENVIRONMENTS

Opuntia

Better known by the name prickly pear, the *Opuntia* has thick racquet-shaped stems with a hard, waxy coating. The leaves are reduced to spines, which limits evaporation.

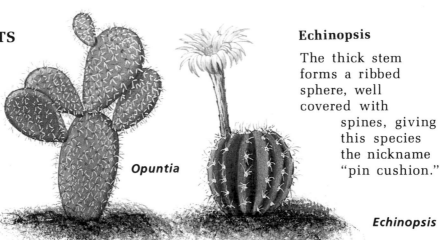

Opuntia

Echinopsis

The thick stem forms a ribbed sphere, well covered with spines, giving this species the nickname "pin cushion."

Echinopsis

SALTY ENVIRONMENTS

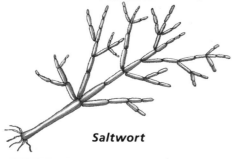

Saltwort

Saltwort

This plant, which grows in salty environments, has fleshy stems capable of storing freshwater. It does not have leaves, and its stems are made of sections placed end to end. Thanks to its thick, waxy epidermis, it can resist the salty water and the assault of the tides.

PLANTS TRANSPIRE

Water is absorbed by the roots, circulates around the plant through the vascular tissues and evaporates (transpires) at the level of the leaves. This release of water creates a vacuum in the vascular tissue, causing a pulling force, which makes the water rise again (rising sap). Thanks to its leaves, the plant acts as a pump which absorbs, pushes out, and breathes in water.

Cover a geranium branch that includes a leaf with a transparent plastic bag and close it with a string. In summer, it only takes a few minutes to see the inner surface of the bag covered with condensation and sprinkled with drops of water.

DID YOU KNOW?

Plants humidify the air by transpiring. In a day, a potted plant throws off about 50 ml (1.7 oz.) of water; a lone tree, 500 liters (473 quarts); a hectare (2.5 acres) of forest, 30 000 liters (28 390 quarts).

PLANTS BREATHE

Just as people and animals do, plants breathe night and day. They absorb oxygen from the air and emit carbon dioxide. But it is difficult to see plants breathing in the daylight, because the exchanges of gas are hidden by other exchanges relating to photosynthesis (see p. 20).

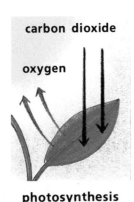

carbon dioxide

oxygen

carbon dioxide

oxygen

photosynthesis during the day

respiration, day and night

GROWING PLANTS WITHOUT SOIL

In cultivation without soil (or hydroponic cultivation), plants are grown in water that contains all the nutrients necessary to their development (nitrogen, phosphorus, potassium plus trace elements such as iron, magnesium oxide, zinc). Each plant species has its special solution. Computers continuously adjust and give the solutions, depending on the needs of the plants and the climatic conditions around them.

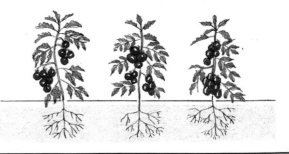

ROOTS DOWNWARD, STEMS UPWARD

Roots grow downward and stems upward. This phenomenon is called *geotropism*, from the Greek *geos*, earth, and *tropos*, direction, meaning "directed toward the Earth."

Soak a few runner beans overnight.

Roll up a piece of paper towel and put it inside a transparent jar that has a cover.

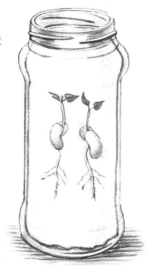

Put the beans between the glass and the paper, and keep the paper moist.

After three days, roots will appear and will turn downward. A little shoot, the stemlet, will also appear, growing upward.

When the little roots measure 1½ inches (4 cm) long, close the jar and turn it upside down.

Several days later, you will notice that the direction of growth of the roots and the stemlets has changed. The stemlets once again are developing upward and the roots are again growing downward.

LOOKING AT THE STOMATES OF A LEEK UNDER THE MICROSCOPE

All the gaseous exchanges between plants and the atmosphere are made through tiny holes called stomates.

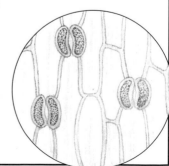

Cut a piece of leaf from a leek and, with the help of a craft knife and tweezers, slice a rectangular piece from its skin. Break it in two; separate the layers until you get a very fine, transparent membrane. Place it on a slide in a drop of water. Cover it with a cover slip and look at it under the microscope.

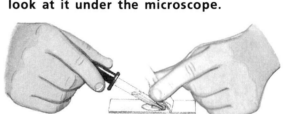

To put the cover slip in place, hold it upright, with one of its sides resting on the slide near the drop. Let it pivot on its edge as you lower it; this way, you avoid the formation of air bubbles between the slide and cover slip.

Between the very elongated cells of the leek epidermis, you can see little holes surrounded by dark shapes like kidney beans. These openings are stomates, which allow the gases that enter and leave the leaf to pass. The dark shapes are the guard cells.

A PLANT IS A FACTORY: PHOTOSYNTHESIS

Plants make their own food: they produce carbohydrates from water, mineral salts, and carbon taken from carbon dioxide with the assistance of sunlight. Among the substances produced by plants we find sugars, starches, and fats (in the seeds), and proteins (see p. 21).

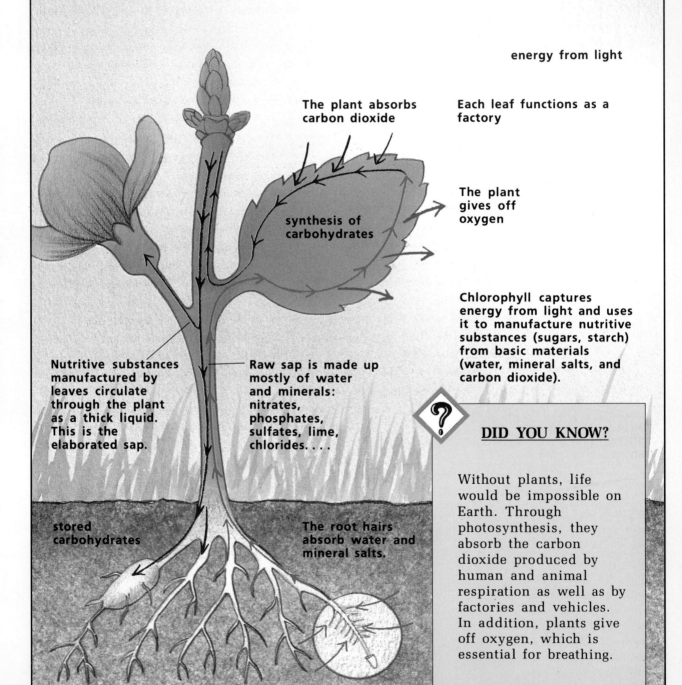

energy from light

The plant absorbs carbon dioxide

Each leaf functions as a factory

synthesis of carbohydrates

The plant gives off oxygen

Chlorophyll captures energy from light and uses it to manufacture nutritive substances (sugars, starch) from basic materials (water, mineral salts, and carbon dioxide).

Nutritive substances manufactured by leaves circulate through the plant as a thick liquid. This is the elaborated sap.

Raw sap is made up mostly of water and minerals: nitrates, phosphates, sulfates, lime, chlorides. . . .

stored carbohydrates

The root hairs absorb water and mineral salts.

DID YOU KNOW?

Without plants, life would be impossible on Earth. Through photosynthesis, they absorb the carbon dioxide produced by human and animal respiration as well as by factories and vehicles. In addition, plants give off oxygen, which is essential for breathing.

CARNIVOROUS PLANTS

Carnivorous plants have the ability to attract, capture, and digest living animal prey, such as flies, mosquitoes, ants. These plants are not satisfied with the classic means of nutrition through photosynthesis. Often living in poor soil, they must complement their diet.

The leaves of the *Drosera* (sundew) are covered with tentacles that secrete a sticky substance in which insects get stuck and are then digested

The Venus's-flytrap *(Dionaea)* imprisons its prey between two racquet-shaped jaws that are capable of closing in a fraction of a second

The ends of *Nepenthes* leaves are pitcher-shaped. Attracted by their color and the nectar they contain, insects fall in and are drowned in the liquid at the bottom of the pitcher

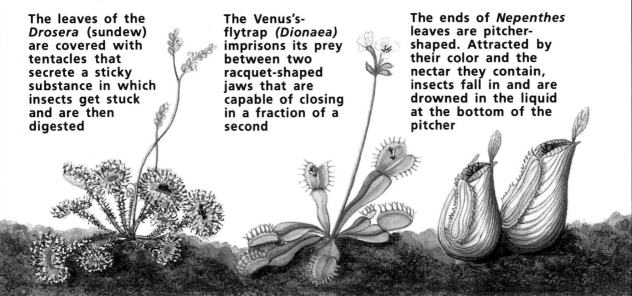

PLANTS AS PRODUCERS

Thanks to photosynthesis, plants produce substances which nourish us.

Sugars such as glucose (grapes, plums), fructose (apples, tomatoes), and sucrose (maple, carrots).

Starch contained in cereals or in starchy foods (corn, rice, beans) or in the tubers of the potato.

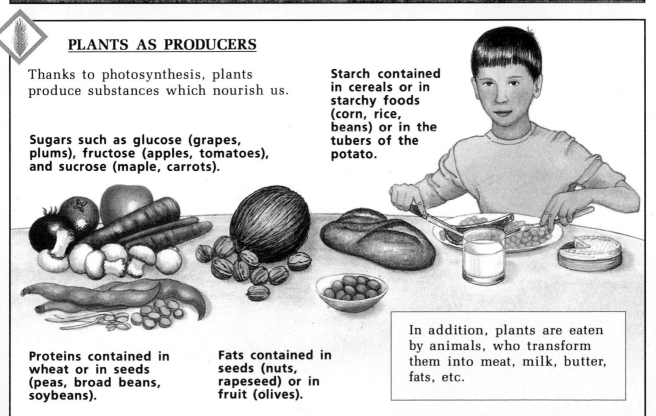

Proteins contained in wheat or in seeds (peas, broad beans, soybeans).

Fats contained in seeds (nuts, rapeseed) or in fruit (olives).

In addition, plants are eaten by animals, who transform them into meat, milk, butter, fats, etc.

REPRODUCTION IN FLOWERING PLANTS

Plants reproduce in two ways: through flowers (sexual reproduction) or through the production of a new plant from a small piece of another plant (vegetative propagation, see pp. 26–27). Flowers carry the male and female reproductive organs of plants. When a grain of pollen settles on the stigma, it germinates, producing a pollen tube, which penetrates the interior of the ovule. This is fertilization.

Dissect a flower with tweezers

Take off the petals one by one. You will see threadlike parts, fused together at the base: these are the stamens (male organs). The little grains of golden dust at the end make up the pollen.

Remove the stamens and what remains is the pistil (the female organ). Its end, covered in sticky hairs, is called the stigma; at the base, the ovary contains what will become the seeds.

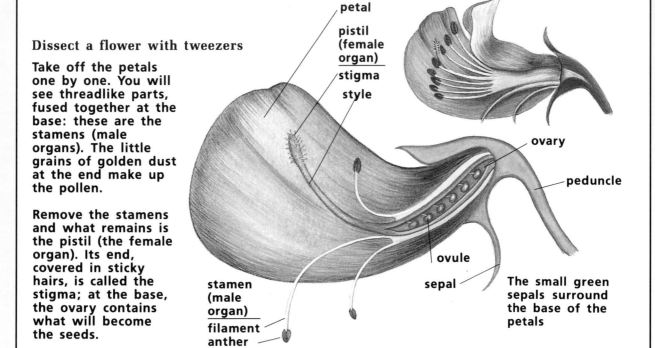

petal

pistil (female organ)

stigma

style

ovary

peduncle

ovule

sepal

stamen (male organ)

filament

anther

The small green sepals surround the base of the petals

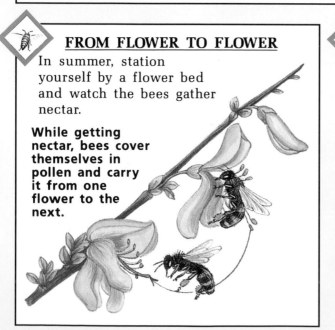

FROM FLOWER TO FLOWER

In summer, station yourself by a flower bed and watch the bees gather nectar.

While getting nectar, bees cover themselves in pollen and carry it from one flower to the next.

LOOKING AT POLLEN UNDER THE MICROSCOPE

Take some grains of pollen from the stamens of a flower and look at them under the microscope. They are tiny. The largest grain is less than 0.2 mm (.0008 in) in diameter.

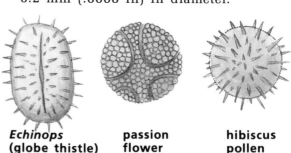

Echinops (globe thistle) pollen

passion flower pollen

hibiscus pollen

THE FLOWER BECOMES FRUIT

After fertilization, the flower is transformed into a fruit. The petals, now useless, dry out and fall off. The ovary becomes a fruit, which surrounds and protects the seeds.

The cherry is a fleshy fruit called a drupe. It contains a tough pit, which protects the seed.

The strawberry is an aggregate fruit. The fleshy mass is sweet and has tiny fruits, or achenes, which form brown spots on the surface.

The berry never opens on its own. The seeds are not released and cannot germinate until after the decomposition of the fruit.

The hazel tree has the male flowers (catkins producing pollen) and the female flowers (the tiny red rosettes) on the same stalk.

FRUITS CONTAIN SEEDS

Take the seeds out of the fruits and vegetables you eat: melon, green pepper, eggplant, or cucumber.

Put them in a strainer and rinse them under water to rid them of pulp. Dry them on a paper towel and sort them into paper packets, on which you have written their names and the date you pack them. Keep your packets in a cool, dry place. Plant your seeds in the spring.

THE DISPERSAL OF SEEDS

Flowering plants have efficient ways to spread their seeds and colonize new spaces.

Vetches explode and shoot out their seeds.

Coconuts are transported by sea currents.

Fruits with hooks or thorns catch onto the fur of animals.

The blackbird eats ivy berries, the mistle thrush likes those of the mistletoe. Dropped on the ground or excreted, the seeds germinate.

MAKING SEEDS GERMINATE

Have fun making seeds of different species germinate. You will get sprouts ready to eat, or green plants, or little trees . . .

Soybeans

Buy some raw soybeans at a health food store and soak them in water for 24 hours. Set them on a cloth napkin placed on a plate. Fold the napkin accordion style, putting a layer of beans in each fold. Water regularly.

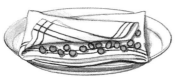

Gather the sprouts when they are 2 inches (4–6 cm) tall. The beans, sprouts and roots, can be eaten raw in a salad or cooked for 5 minutes in salted boiling water.

Avocado pit

Wash your pit and let it soak in water for 2 or 3 days.

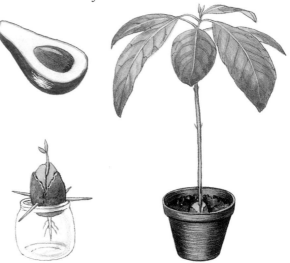

Support it with toothpicks. Add water regularly so that the bottom of the pit stays wet. Two months afterwards, when the seedling has 6 leaves, plant it in a pot with pebbles at the bottom and filled with a mixture of ⅔ potting soil and ⅓ sand. Water regularly and fertilize twice a year.

CAT SNACK

Line the bottom of a tray with a thick layer of paper towels. Get some uncooked wheat berries. Draw a cat's head in permanent marker. Wet the towels.

At the end of one week, the shoots are ready to be cut for a salad . . . or for your cat!

Place the wheat berries on the paper one by one, following the lines, without space between them.

Keep the paper towel very moist; spray it with water, so you don't disturb the seeds.

After two or three days, the seeds begin to grow, and the tops of the shoots reproduce the outline of your cat face.

GROWING A TREE

Gather some acorns, making sure there are no worms inside. In order to remove the shells that protect the kernels, you must subject the acorns to a treatment called stratification.

Stratification

• Place a thin layer of gravel followed by a layer of sand in the bottom of a pot.
• Put in the acorns and cover them with sand.
• Water and cover your pot with a board held in place by a stone.
• Place your pot in a cool, dark place and water it two to three times a week.

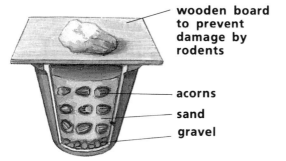

wooden board to prevent damage by rodents

acorns

sand

gravel

You can use the same method for other very hard pits.

date   peach   apricot

Several weeks after stratification, your sprouted acorns are ready for planting.

Fill a pot with a layer of gravel at the bottom and a mixture of half potting soil and half peat. Gently remove an acorn from the stratification pot and set it near the top of the new pot. Cover it with sieved potting soil.

sieved potting soil

sprouted acorn

gravel

mixture of half potting soil, half peat

Once the seedling appears, water it two to three times a week and keep it in the light. The oak will put out its first leaves. One year later, put it in a bigger pot. When it is 27 in. (70 cm) tall, transplant it somewhere far from your garden and water well.

VEGETATIVE PROPAGATION

Plants mostly reproduce by seeds. But they can also reproduce from small pieces of the plants' stem, root, leaf, bud, or shoot. Put in the earth, the cutting develops its own roots and produces a new plant identical to that from which it came.

Certain plants—for example, the strawberry—put out runners that produce new plants.

TAKING A CUTTING FROM A SPIDER PLANT

The spider plant develops long stems with young plantlets, which are good for cuttings. Cut the stem ¾ inch (2 cm) from the base of a young plant.

Take off the bottom leaves of the plantlet and plant it in a pot of potting soil. Water regularly. Cover the pot with a transparent plastic bag to keep the new plant moist.

TAKING A CUTTING FROM THE LEAF OF A *BEGONIA REX*

The *Begonia* rex lends itself particularly well to the technique of flat leaf cuttings.
1. Fill a deep tray with peat and take a beautiful begonia leaf. Place it flat on the potting soil, veins down. Make six to ten cuts along the veins with a knife. Water.

2. At the end of three weeks, roots and leaf buds will appear at the places you cut. When the leaves are 5 cm (2 inches) tall, cut them apart with a knife, separating them from the original leaf without damaging their roots.

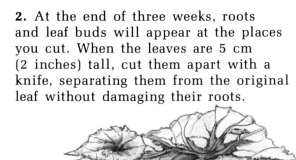

3. Place each new plant in a pot filled with peat and water it regularly.

TAKING A CUTTING FROM A GERANIUM STEM

1. On a geranium, mark off two or three nice pieces of stem, each with at least two pairs of leaves and a bud at the top. Cut each off below a leaf as shown at left.

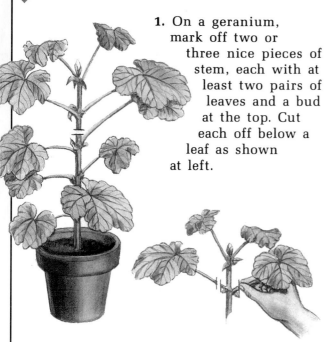

2. Take off the two leaves at the base of each bud and dip them in a hormone rooting powder, purchased at a garden supply store.

3. Fill a pot with pebbles at the bottom and then add a half sand, half potting soil mixture. Plant your cuttings. Pack the earth tightly and water regularly.

hormone rooting powder

4. Place it in the light, and water it. Cover the pot in a transparent plastic bag pierced with several holes.

5. After about 20 days, remove the bag. If the leaves are healthy, repot the plant in a larger pot, filled with fresh potting soil.

TAKING A CUTTING FROM A MINT ROOT

Mint has a network of interlacing underground roots. Pull up a plant in the garden and cut a few pieces that have rootlets and buds. Each of those pieces is a root cutting which only wants to grow into a new mint plant.

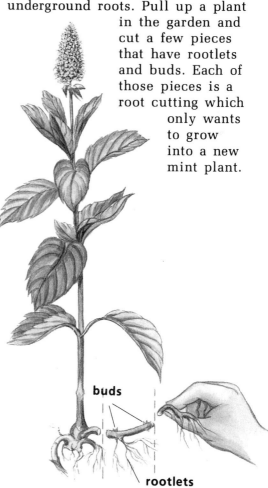

buds

rootlets

Bury the cuttings in a pot filled with potting soil and water regularly.

After several weeks, a new plant will emerge from the soil.

PREPARING YOUR GARDEN

When you make a garden, you challenge the laws of nature. It is rare for a plant to naturally find enough nourishing soil, moisture, and warmth to grow. With patience and care, people have learned to grow beautiful flowers and vegetables. Profit from this knowledge: prepare the earth well and maintain it. Devote a little time to it every day. Encourage animals that are friendly to gardens to visit: they will help you keep away the ones that want to eat the young shoots!

GARDENS IN THE FRENCH AND ENGLISH STYLES

In the 17th century, architects such as André Le Nôtre invented French gardens, with vast flower beds in geometric patterns. Later on, in the so-called English gardens, an effort was made to recreate the landscape in its natural state by mingling shrubbery and flowering bushes.

French garden

THE GARDENER'S OUTFIT AND TOOLS

straw hat

gardening gloves

basket

apron with pocket

old jeans

boots

wheelbarrow

FOR SOWING AND PLANTING

small shovel   **hand rake**   **garden trowel**

dibble   **gardener's line**   **sieve**

FOR WORKING THE EARTH AND WEEDING

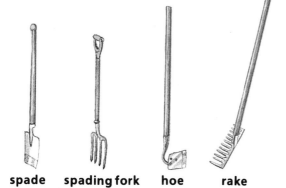

spade   **spading fork**   **hoe**   **rake**

FOR PRUNING AND WATERING

pruning shears

shears   **watering can**

MAKING A GARDENER'S LINE

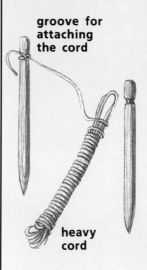

groove for attaching the cord

heavy cord

The line helps you to align your plantings. Sharpen one end of each of two wooden sticks and make a groove around the other end. In the grooves, tie a cord the length of the flower bed you want, and roll the line up on one of the stakes.

MAKING YOUR MINI-GREENHOUSE

A mini-greenhouse will let you start the seedlings indoors that you will plant out in your garden or in pots later on.

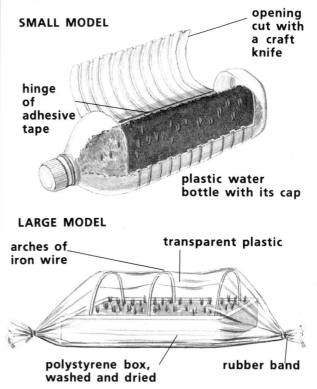

SMALL MODEL

opening cut with a craft knife

hinge of adhesive tape

plastic water bottle with its cap

LARGE MODEL

arches of iron wire   **transparent plastic**

polystyrene box, washed and dried   **rubber band**

MAKING A PLAN FOR YOUR GARDEN

Choose a piece of flat ground, easy to get to and without trees so that your plantings will not be in the shade. For each kind of flower or vegetable, note on your plan the dates you plant your seedlings and when you do each procedure to them.

Borders of flower beds around the beds of vegetables and herbs are both decorative and useful.

Add a shed for your tools and your gardening supplies.

A large empty can or barrel will let you collect rainwater if you do not have running water nearby.

Line up several red currant, black currant, and raspberry plants along a wall or fence. Space them about 5 feet (1.5 meters) apart.

Mark off the garden sections with the help of your gardener's line so that they'll be well aligned.

Don't make your plots too large. You should be able to get to your crops without stepping on any plants.

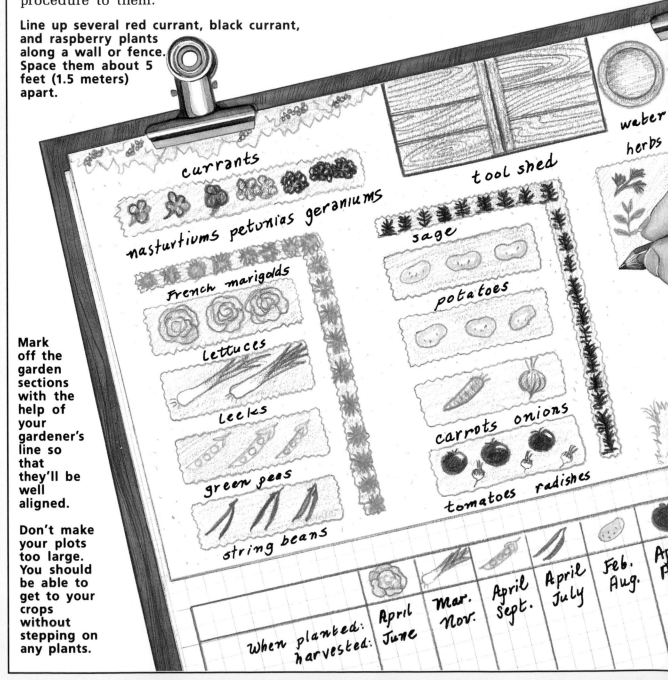

currants

nasturtiums petunias geraniums

tool shed

water

herbs

French marigolds

sage

Lettuces

potatoes

Leeks

green peas

carrots onions

string beans

tomatoes radishes

When planted: April   Mar.   April   April   Feb.   Ap
harvested: June   Nov.   Sept.   July   Aug.

30

A test plot for growing wild plants: after several years, you can make a thick border of wild plants; take care to grow the small ones in front of the big ones. Don't let harmful or invasive plants such as nettles, couch grass, or chickweed take over your garden.

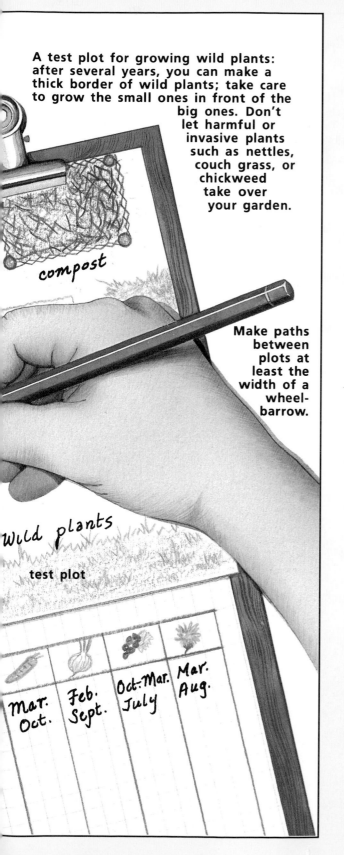

compost

Make paths between plots at least the width of a wheelbarrow.

wild plants

test plot

Mar. Oct. Feb. Sept. Oct.-Mar. July Mar. Aug.

GATHERING WILD PLANTS FOR YOUR TEST PLOT

In the spring, go through the countryside looking for young plants that you know or you can identify with the help of a guidebook. Be sure not to take any endangered species.

Cut out the clump of earth surrounding the plant with a knife, lift it up with a dibble, and put it in a plastic bag. Quickly replant it in your garden and water it.

In autumn, go hunting for seeds, store them in a dry, dark place, and sow them in the spring.

small paper packets

name of the plant

date gathered

place gathered

poppy

7.10.96

Hill Rd.

A FEW COMMON WILD FLOWERS

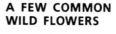

violet   primrose   cornflower

poppy   evening primrose   willow-herb   lily-of-the-valley

LOOKING AFTER YOUR GARDEN

1. *Watering.* Using your dibble, dig down about 2 inches (5 cm) into the earth to make sure it is nice and moist. Use your watering can with its spray head. Don't overwater: too much water strangles plants.

2. *Hoeing.* "A good hoeing is worth two waterings," gardeners say. Using a hoe, break the crust which forms on the surface of the earth. This way, you help aerate the soil and keep the water from evaporating.

3. *Weeding.* Weeds multiply at the beginning of summer. If you remove them by weeding regularly, they will become less and less frequent. Gently pull them up the day after watering, so that you will get the roots.

4. *Fertilizing.* Avoid using chemical fertilizers, as they pollute. Use a natural fertilizer, compost, which you can make with decomposed plant matter.

1

2

3

4

MAKING YOUR OWN COMPOST

Compost is a natural product, made by the decomposition of vegetable waste in the garden in a compost heap. In a corner of your garden, lay out a small enclosure where you will accumulate vegetable debris: cut grass, dead leaves, twigs, fruit and vegetable peelings and wood ash. Enrich this debris with manure and water it two to three times a week. Turn it regularly with a spading fork.

After three months, your compost is ready. Use it to add nutrients to your garden and improve the soil texture. Remove it from the bottom of the pile and continue to throw new waste on top.

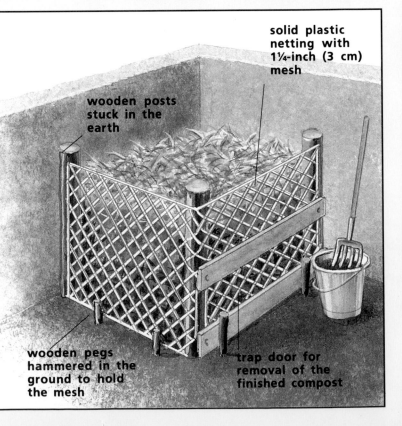

solid plastic netting with 1¼-inch (3 cm) mesh

wooden posts stuck in the earth

wooden pegs hammered in the ground to hold the mesh

trap door for removal of the finished compost

RAISING EARTHWORMS

Earthworms aid in the decomposition of organic matter and aerate the soil.

You can watch them at work and judge the results by making a small earthworm farm in a bottle.

MATERIALS

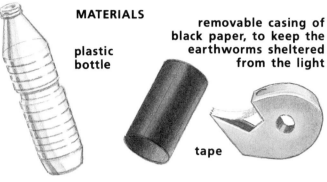

plastic bottle

removable casing of black paper, to keep the earthworms sheltered from the light

tape

scouring pad

earthworms

craft knife

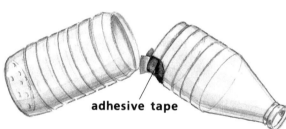

With a craft knife, cut off the neck of the bottle and tape one of the sides with adhesive tape to make a hinge.

adhesive tape

Pierce several holes in the bottom of the bottle for drainage and line it with a clean, soapless scouring pad. Place gravel or clay aggregate balls in the bottom; then add alternating layers of sand and compost. Water the surface well, and put in six nice earthworms from your garden.

potting soil

river sand

gravel or clay pellets

scouring pad (for a barrier)

Set a layer of decomposed dead leaves on top and water daily with a plant mister. Cover the bottle with the paper casing; you can slide it up to watch the earthworms in action.

dead leaves

After several months you will note that all the layers have been stirred up, mixed, and loosened. Earthworms bury and eat the plant particles they come across on the way. These are then excreted and transformed into smaller particles, which plants can use.

STARTING YOUR FLOWER AND VEGETABLE SEEDLINGS INDOORS

Sowing is the process of putting a seed in soil so that it can germinate. At the end of winter, you can sow vegetable and flower seeds indoors. Once the seedlings have grown a little, you can replant them—first in pots, then in the garden. This way, you get stronger plants.

tomato   marigold   sage

Tamp down the earth with your hand or with a plasterer's hawk to make a smooth surface before scattering the seeds.

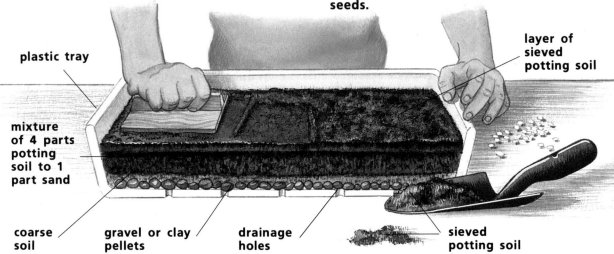

plastic tray

layer of sieved potting soil

mixture of 4 parts potting soil to 1 part sand

coarse soil

gravel or clay pellets

drainage holes

sieved potting soil

1. Sow the smallest seeds by strewing them; space the largest ones 1 inch (2 cm) apart. Cover them with sieved potting soil and tamp down.

2. For ten minutes, soak the tray in a basin or a bowl of water. (Direct watering would disturb the seeds.)

3. Cover your tray with clear plastic film and

place it by a window away from direct sunlight. Turn it every day to keep the seedlings from leaning to one side. Water regularly.

4. When the plants sprout real leaves, transplant them to a larger tray. Set them out in staggered rows, an inch (2 or 3 cm) apart. After a few weeks, transplant them to the garden (see p. 35).

SOWING YOUR SEEDS OUTDOORS

Choose plants that are hardy such as radishes, beans, carrots, nasturtiums, and sweet peas.

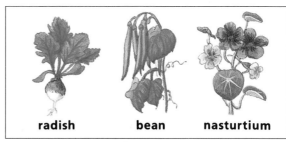

radish   bean   nasturtium

1. Prepare the ground in order to get a fine texture: remove stones and weeds with a hand cultivator and go over it with a rake. If the ground is dry, soften it by watering it the evening before.

2. Trace a good straight line using your gardener's line and make a furrow the length of the string with the edge of your plasterer's hawk or with a stick. Strew two or three seeds at regular intervals and cover them over lightly. It is enough for them to be covered by earth two or three times the seeds' thickness. The smaller the seeds, the thinner the covering layer of earth. Tamp down the earth with your plasterer's hawk or a flat piece of wood, and water the seedlings.

3. As the plants get bigger, they will get in each other's way because they are too close together. Thin out the weakest ones after having watered the earth to soften it. Hold the earth in place around the plant with one hand and gently pull it out with the other hand. Make sure to pat down the earth around the plants you leave in place.

TRANSPLANTING TO THE GARDEN

Prepare the earth so that it is fine and soft, and rid it of stones and weeds. Trace a line with your gardener's line and make a furrow with the edge of your plasterer's hawk. Plan a space between each plant. Make a hole with the dibble, put in the plant, add earth, and tamp it down. Dig another hole next to the plant so you can pat down the earth at the level of the roots; water through this hole.

Water regularly, preferably in the evening. Remove weeds. Don't sow seeds or transplant during the heat of the day.

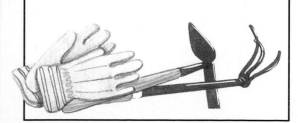

THE GARDEN IN SUMMER

A brief daily visit to your garden will let you remove weeds, cut wilted flowers, and especially, check the growth of all the plants, flowers, fruits and vegetables. Wait until evening to water, so you don't burn your plants.

red currant

blackcurrant

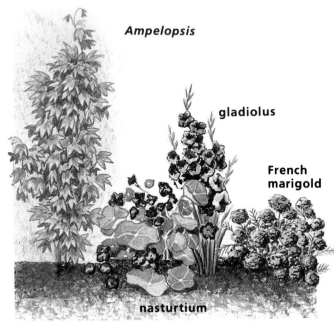

Ampelopsis

gladiolus

French marigold

nasturtium

Leeks: cut the ends of their greenery and build up the earth around each plant in order to get the largest possible white part.

Gladioli tend to bend over once they reach a certain height. A few stakes, a cord tied around them at the right height, or a horizontal lattice work will help keep them upright.

leek

onion

carrot

Taste the raw green beans: they snap in your teeth; don't wait for them to make strings to harvest them.

green beans

green peas

Onions: Cut the ends of their leaves. Underground, the bulbs will become larger.

Carrots: remove one out of every two plants in order to allow the remaining carrots to get nice and big.

Strawberries, currants, raspberries, and blackcurrants turn red at the beginning of summer. Taste them before picking. If they are still bitter, be patient for another few days before picking them.

potatoes   lettuce

Potatoes: once flowers appear, pile little mounds of earth around each plant to protect the young tubers from the light and increase the chances of their multiplying.

Tomatoes, green peas and runner beans: insert a stake to one side of each plant to keep them from spreading out across the ground. Gradually, as the stem grows longer, attach it to the stake with fairly wide ties (like pieces of flat raffia).

Lettuce: in dry weather, water them often to keep them from getting gritty.

tomatoes

A DRIED-FLOWER SCRAPBOOK

On a nice summer day, gather some wild flowers. Choose the prettiest specimens, including flowers, fruits, and roots if possible. Place them in a large box without crushing them and take them back home as quickly as possible. Place each plant flat in a sheath of newspaper, which you should change every three days.

sheath of newspaper

Take several pieces of corrugated cardboard and two wooden boards. Alternate the plants and the cardboard pieces. Press them together by putting a strap or belt around them.

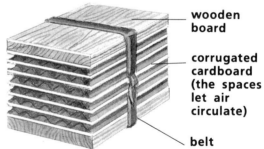

wooden board

corrugated cardboard (the spaces let air circulate)

belt

Three weeks later, carefully attach each dried plant to a sheet of drawing paper with tape or glue. Identify the name of the plant, its family, and the place and date you picked it, punch holes, and put it in a looseleaf; you've made a dried flower scrapbook, or *herbarium*.

THE LIFE CYCLE

Annuals germinate, flower, make seeds and die in one year.

poppy   **nasturtium**   **French marigold**

Biennials have a life cycle spread out over two years: the first year they grow and stock food reserves in their roots. The following year, they flower and make seeds.

Queen Anne's lace   **salsify**   **burdock**

Perennials live for several years, developing deep roots

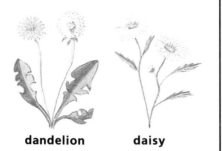

dandelion   **daisy**

MAKING BULBS FLOWER IN WINTER

In October, buy some large bulbs of narcissus, hyacinth, crocus, or daffodil for forcing. Place them in labelled plastic bags and put them in the bottom of the refrigerator. After six weeks, you can make them flower.

hyacinth bulb

The bottom of the bulb should be about ½-inch (1 cr above the water.

In water

Put a hyacinth bulb in the neck of a glass carafe filled with water. Put the carafe in a cool, dark place.

When the shoots are 2 to 4 inches (5 to 10 cm) tall, take the carafe out into the light. The warmer it is, the sooner the plant will blossom.

EVERY SEASON HAS ITS FLOWERS

Change your plants according to the season.

SPRING   **SUMMER**

grape hyacinth   **tulip**   **crocus**   **petunia**   **sage**   **marigold**

WINTER

You can use the same tub to make a window box for winter. Place it indoors, in the light, and plant an assortment of green plants.

begonia   *Tradescantia*   **African violet**

In a bed of pebbles

Choose a waterproof container at least 4 inches (10 cm) deep. Fill it halfway with pebbles or clay aggregate pellets. Place the bulbs, pointed ends up, on the bed of pebbles or pellets and push them in a little so they will have some support. Then put in more pellets or pebbles. Fill with water. Put the container in a cool, dark place; move it into the warmth and light when the shoots are 2 inches (5 cm) tall.

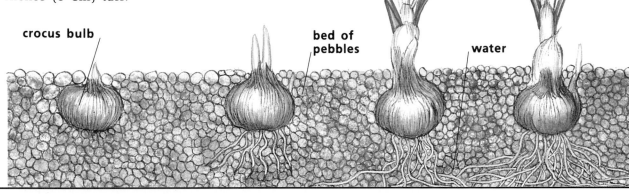

crocus bulb

bed of pebbles

water

A WINDOW BOX

Floral window boxes, usually long and narrow, are meant to be placed outdoors. Buy seedlings with their clumps of earth in trays and transplant them with a dibble, putting the tallest at the center and the shorter ones at the sides.

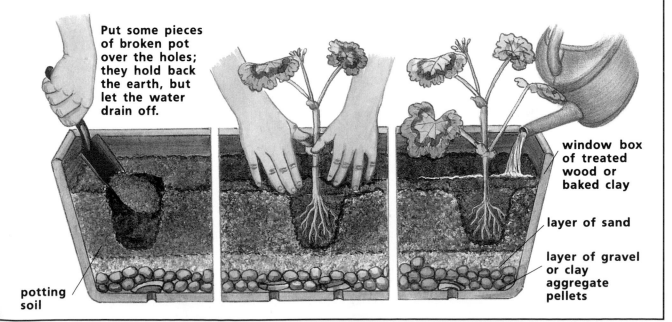

Put some pieces of broken pot over the holes; they hold back the earth, but let the water drain off.

window box of treated wood or baked clay

layer of sand

layer of gravel or clay aggregate pellets

potting soil

GARDEN ANIMALS

Certain animals who live in the garden can do a great deal of damage by feeding on the plants or by carrying diseases. Several insects and numerous birds will help you rid yourself of these many, often invisible pests. Certain flowering plants act as very efficient insecticides for vegetables.

Avoid using chemical insecticides. If you really want to get the better of harmful insects, make your own insecticide! Take a few cloves of garlic, peel them, and crush them with a pestle. Mix them with water and spray this solution on the leaves of your plants.

Put wood ash around your salad plants. It repels slugs.

Moles can rapidly dig long underground tunnels. You can keep them away by planting stakes with empty plastic bottles on them at regular intervals. The bottles move in the wind, making noise, which frightens the moles.

Put ladybugs on plants attacked by aphids.

Encourage insect-eating birds, such as the thrush, robin, swallow, and titmouse, by putting up birdhouses and by giving them seeds to eat (mix wheat and millet).

POLLINATORS

Bees, bumblebees, wasps, and butterflies pollinate flowers. But flies, birds, bats, opossums, and even mice pollinate flowers, too. The wind also carries pollen grains. In summer, clouds of pollen may be seen floating in the air.

Raise certain flowering plants that repel insects. The French marigold and the geranium keep insects from coming near the vegetables. Plant certain things together; for example, mint repels bean flies. Onions repel carrot flies.

Do not chase away bees, wasps, or bumblebees; they pollinate flowers (see p. 22).

Don't squash spiders; they capture many insects in their webs.

GLOSSARY

Angiosperms: literally, *vessel-seed plants*; flowering plants; they produce seeds enclosed in an ovary (fruit).

Annual: a plant that sprouts, flowers, makes seeds, and dies within one year of germination.

Anther: the top part of the stamen; it carries the pollen.

Berry: (1) a fleshy, usually edible fruit that grows on a bush. Examples: currant, strawberry. (2) A simple fruit with a pulpy or fleshy ovary wall, for example a grape or tomato.

Biennial: a plant whose life cycle extends over two years.

Binomial: the scientific name for an organism, which consists of its genus and species names, which frequently have Latin and Greek roots. Each plant has a binomial and also frequently a common name. People all over the world designate species by the same binomials, but the common names of organisms vary from place to place. The binomial system was invented by Carolus Linnaeus in the 18th century.

Bryophytes: simple green plants that lack vascular tissue, true roots, stems, and leaves. Mosses and liverworts are bryophytes.

Bud: a small, compact outgrowth from which branches, leaves, or flowers develop.

Bulb: a modified plant organ, often underground, consisting of a bud, scales, roots, and stored food. From the bulb, the plant can grow its above-ground parts each year.

Calyx: the outer set of floral leaves, consisting of the sepals.

Catkin: a group of flowers containing the male or female parts. It may grow in hanging clusters (for example, the catkin of the hazelnut tree) or be small, more or less rounded and downy (like the pussy willow).

Cellulose: a fibrous substance that forms the walls of cells in plants.

Chlorophyll: the green pigment of plants, which they use to make their food by photosynthesis.

Classification: the way scientists organize living things. The categories of classification are called *taxons*. From the largest to the smallest, the categories are: kingdom, phylum, class, order, family, genus, and species.

Compost: decayed plant matter, used to fertilize and improve soil quality. Gardeners make their own compost by leaving old plant waste in a compost heap.

Cones: Reproductive structures of trees such as pine, spruce, or cedar (conifers), consisting of a mass of scales bearing either ovules (on female cones) or pollen (on male cones). *Conifer* means "carrying cones."

Corolla: the petals of a flower

Cuticle: a waxy layer on the outside of many parts of plants, such as leaves and stems.

Cutting: (n.) a piece (stem, leaf, or root) of a plant that is used to grow a new plant.

Decomposition: decay by the action of bacteria.

Drupe: a fleshy fruit with a hard stone, such as a cherry.

Embryonic plant: the young plant, which develops after fertilization of an ovule. In seed plants, it is contained in the seed and consists of a tiny stem bearing a bud, a root, and seed leaves.

Epidermis: the outer layer of cells of a leaf, stem, or root.

Fertilization: fusion of the male and female sex cells.

Fruit: the ripened, fertilized ovary or ovaries of a flower.

Germination: The early stages of growth of a seed as it becomes a new plant.

Gymnosperms: literally, *naked-seed plants*; a class of plants that includes evergreen conifers, spruces, and hemlocks, many of which carry their seeds on the open scales of cones.

Head: a group of flowers that grow on the stem without a stalk; for example, a clover blossom.

Hormone rooting powder: this powder furthers the formation of roots on cuttings.

Hydroponics: a method of growing plants in a solution of nutrients, instead of in soil.

Inflorescence: the arrangement of flowers on a stem. There are many different shapes of inflorescence.

Insectivorous: insect-eating; able to catch and digest insects.

Lichens: compound plants made up of algae and fungi. They frequently live in harsh environments.

Liverworts: primitive green land plants that have branching leaves that grow flat on moist soil or water. They are part of the phylum Bryophyta. They are often shaped like a liver, which is where they get their name.

Manure: any material that contains nutrients for plants, including animal manures and plant manures.

Nectar: sweet liquid secreted by flowers, and used by bees in the production of honey.

Node: part of a stem where one or more leaves arise.

Ovary: organ of the flower forming the lower part of the pistil and enclosing the ovules.

Ovule: structure contained in the ovary which, after fertilization of the egg-cell within it, may develop into a seed.

Peduncle: the stalk of an inflorescence.

Petiole: a leaf stalk.

Photosynthesis: the process by which green plants use energy from sunlight to make their own food from simpler materials

Pigment: substance that gives color to certain plant tissues. Chlorophyll is a pigment.

Pips: small seeds contained in certain fleshy fruits (pear, melon, apple, orange, grape).

Pistil: the female organ of a flower, consisting of the stigma, style (stalk), and ovary.

Plant: (1) a young tree, vine, shrub, or herb, suitable for planting; (2) a member of the plant kingdom; plants make their own food by photosynthesis, don't move around on their own, have cellulose in their cell walls, and share other characteristics.

Pollen: a powdery mass of tiny spores containing the male sex cells of a seed plant, which is produced in the anthers.

Pollen tube: very tiny tube put out by the pollen grain, which penetrates the stigma and carries the male sex cells to the egg.

Pollination: transfer of pollen from an anther to a stigma. Bees and other pollinating insects that fly from flower to flower in order to take nectar and pollen aid in pollination.

Proteins: naturally occurring compounds made up of carbon, hydrogen, oxygen, nitrogen, and sulfur that are basic parts of all living cells.

Rhizome: underground stem, bearing buds that can become new plants by means of vegetative propagation.

Root hairs: tiny hairlike structures on a root surface that help to absorb water.

Rootlet: secondary branching of a root; a small root.

Seed: the ripened ovule produced by a flowering plant as a result of fertilization, which contains an embryo that can grow into an adult plant.

Seed bed: the place where one has sown seeds.

Sepals: the modified leaves that make up the calyx of a flower, which protect the bud and surround the petals of the flower.

Sowing: the action of putting seeds in the ground.

Spores: tiny reproductive cells present in mushrooms, mosses, and ferns.

Sprout: the shoot of a plant, from a seed or tuber.

Stamen: the male organ of a flowering plant, consisting of a stalk or filament, and an anther, which produces the pollen.

Starch: the main storage form of carbohydrates in plants.

Stemlet: a small, slender young stem.

Stigma: the upper, free surface of the pistil (the female plant organ), on which grains of pollen stick.

Stolon: a horizontally growing stem that develops from a bud, and is able to root at the nodes to produce a new plant. The strawberry produces stolons. Also known as a *runner*.

Tendril: corkscrew-shaped filament put out by climbing plants such as vines. Some tendrils are modified stems; some are modified leaves.

Trace elements: chemical elements (for example, zinc, boron, or iodine) present in small quantities in plant tissues, which are essential for their life processes.

Tracheophytes: literally, *tube plants*; plants with a system of tubelike structures for conducting water.

Includes ferns, gymnosperms, and angiosperms.

Tuber: swollen, underground outgrowth of certain plants; it may be an outgrowth of the stem or the roots. Tubers carry buds that can grow into new plants by vegetative propagation. Examples: potato, dahlia.

Vegetative propagation: asexual reproduction that happens when a part of the plant (like a leaf, rhizome, bulb or stem) is cut off and develops into a new plant.

Vetch: a group of herblike annuals that bear fruit that are legumes. Broad beans belong to the vetch family.

INDEX